Donor Conception Network

Telling and Talking with family and friends about donor conception: A Guide for Parents

By
Olivia Montuschi

Olivia Montuschi

Olivia Montuschi is the mother of two donor conceived young people, born in 1983 and 1986. She and her husband Walter Merricks founded the Donor Conception Network with four other families in 1993. Olivia trained as a teacher and a counsellor and for many years worked as a parenting educator and trainer, writing materials and running parenting education programmes. She now works part-time as Practice Consultant to DC Network.

Donor Conception Network

**© Donor Conception Network, April 2006.
Updated August 2012 and May 2015.**

All rights reserved. You are welcome to reproduce all or part of this booklet as long as you acknowledge the source.

ISBN 978-1-910222-27-0

Published by the
Donor Conception Network,
154 Caledonian Road, London N1 9RD

Telephone: 020 7278 2608
email: enquiries@dcnetwork.org
www.dcnetwork.org

Contents

Methodology
Acknowledgements and thanks

Introduction — 1

Why do other people need to know? — 2

Becoming an educator — 2
- Avoidance v curiosity — 3

When to tell — 5
- Telling others before the child understands — 5
- Before treatment — 6
- During treatment — 7
- Avoiding painful events — 7
- Pregnancy — 7
- After a child is born — 8
- Second stage telling — 9

Who to tell — 9
- Parents — 10
- Letting go of the need for approval — 11
- Recognising our parent's life experience — 11
- Siblings — 12
- Friends — 13
- Other children in the extended family or children of friends — 14
- If I tell others how can I control the information? — 16
- Once my child knows can I have influence over who s/he tells? — 16
- Solo mums and lesbian couples: when family type is the dominant issue — 18

How much to tell — 20

Reflections on telling — 21
- When the response is negative — 22

Final thoughts — 24

Dos and don'ts — 25

Resources — 26
- Books — 26
- Films — 26
- Research on sharing information with others — 27

Organisations — 28
- Useful websites — 29

Methodology

This booklet, and Our Family, the companion volume for relatives and friends, was a long time in the making. It was August 2009 when the idea of writing something to help parents and would-be parents share information about donor conception with friends and family was first mooted in the Donor Conception Network's (DCN or DC Network) eBulletin. The response from members and mental health professionals from all over the world was enthusiastic. Everyone was beginning to notice that telling relatives and friends about the use of donor conception in family building was now felt by many people to be more difficult than sharing information with donor conceived children.

DC Network celebrated its twentieth birthday in 2013. As one of the founders I feel privileged to have spoken with many thousands of families over these years. This, plus my own experience of being part of a donor conception family for 30 years informs my general approach to this booklet. In addition, in special preparation for writing about this particular topic, I researched the literature currently available about sharing information on general infertility, bereavement, cancer, mental illness etc. with family and friends. The research literature on the sharing of information about donor conception is small and well known to me. It has, however, been enriched by the Relative Strangers project conducted between 1st October 2010 and 30th June 2013 by the Morgan Centre at Manchester University and these booklets have benefitted from the findings. DC Network also ran a national conference on Talking with Family and Friends and at this I organised an exercise to help members think around the subject. This resulted in over 100 written responses and many email addresses inviting me to follow up with a personal interview.

Acknowledgements and thanks

Enormous thanks go first of all to the Nuffield Foundation without whose funding support this booklet would have remained a wish rather than a reality.

I am indebted to DC Network members Jane Ellis, Ruth Yudkin, Caroline Spencer, Marion Scott and Natasha Canfer for their very constructive comments on and additions to the text as it emerged. Both the content and the way it is expressed improved immeasurably as a result. Thanks also to Marion for additional mentoring services. Final thanks to my beloved husband Walter who writes so beautifully himself and whose fluent command of the English language drives me to despair and admiration in equal parts.

The people without whom this booklet would not have been possible are those DC Network members who took part in the Fears and Successes exercise at the national conference in September 2012, and particularly those of you I met or spoke to on the phone over the following months. Also those members who responded to my request in DCN's eBulletin for people willing to talk with me on this topic. Thank you all very much for being so generous with your time and stories. By contributing to this booklet you are almost certainly helping many, many others feel more comfortable and confident about talking with family and friends.

Telling and talking with family and friends about donor conception

"Donor conception has given us two wonderful children and we're happy to tell people about it, but it's not the most important thing about our family."

Introduction

Welcome to this booklet, which is intended as a support for all potential and actual parents of young donor conceived children. The focus is on deciding who else needs to know about the help you are having or have already had in creating your family; the why, when, who and how much of sharing information in the best interests of your children and the whole family.

Over the next few pages you will find reasons why it is helpful for your children that close family and friends know about donor conception and an exploration of why it is that being open with relatives and friends can sometimes feel so difficult. Throughout there are stories and quotes from real families, parents-to-be and mums and dads. There are also lots of practical suggestions and a check list of ways in which you can help others respond to you in the most appropriate and supportive ways.

Although in-vitro-fertilisation (IVF) has largely become a well-understood and accepted way to conceive a child, donor conception remains a 'different' way for a child to come into a family. Another person (or persons), usually not identified at the time of conception, has been involved in assisting that child to come into being. This resulted in the long history of secrecy that has surrounded donor conception. Historically, men and women have often felt guilt and shame about infertility and their need to use eggs, sperm or embryos from another person to create their family. It is not so long ago that many doctors strongly advised patients not to mention their treatment to anyone. These days it is not just infertile couples who are using donor eggs or sperm for family building. Single women and lesbian couples are successfully raising families created with donor help. Increasingly parents in all family types are understanding that openness with children is healthier for the whole family than secrecy, even if some still struggle with actually starting to tell. What seems to remain for many is fear of judgement and sometimes rejection by relatives and friends.

In the research I conducted amongst DC Network members at a national conference prior to writing this booklet, the terms embarrassment (causing this in others or worrying that children would feel this way), judgement, rejection and difference were mentioned many times as fears. However, very few of those who took part reported that these fears had materialised.

Several members mentioned that the act of talking with friends had deepened their own understanding of what it means to become a parent by donor conception. Sharing information also resulted in a very rewarding strengthening of trust within the friendship. Taking charge of the information, making positive decisions about who should know and how this should happen, seemed to help many people build confidence and feel in control.

Telling and talking with family and friends about donor conception

Why do other people need to know?

Openness with children about donor conception is, as I am writing in mid 2013, now more usual than secrecy, at least in the UK. It is widely acknowledged that parents who are confident and comfortable about the choices they have made are more likely to feel that it is in the best interest of their children and the whole family that information starts to be shared before a child is five. This doesn't necessarily make it any easier to begin to do this and many parents remain anxious about first using even the simple language contained in the *Our Story* books. Most do get the words out in the end and then continue with increasing confidence as children carry on as normal with no negative reactions.

When a child begins to gain an understanding of what they are being told – and this could vary in age from about four to seven or eight – they may start to talk about it with relatives and friends. This is the main reason that many people gave me as to why their close relatives and friends also need to know.

> "We could just imagine her telling granny about the 'nice lady who gave mummy an egg to help make me', so it was important to us that granny was told about egg donation long before this could happen."
> *Stephanie, mum to Millie two and a half*

Another reason for talking early with family and close friends is that conversations about likenesses – and these come up all the time in families – can be responded to truthfully and potentially with some humour. Unshared information can become a barrier to relationships that could be supportive for you. Sharing information in a matter of fact way usually means that donor conception can take a proportionate place in family life. Mostly it takes up no space at all, but just needs taking out and dusting off from time to time. If you cannot tell those close to you about the different way in which your child has come into the family, it could mean that at some level it has remained a big issue for you and that there may be some feelings of shame or embarrassment associated with it. If this is so then it may be difficult for your child to feel proud about being donor conceived. These feelings would ideally be resolved before treatment starts but it is never too late to re-visit them with the help of a good friend, someone at DC Network or a counsellor.

Becoming an educator

One of the unexpected roles that parents by donor conception can find themselves falling in to is that of educator. You may resist this at first, feeling that it is hard enough having to make difficult decisions for yourself, let alone explain them to others. But I encourage you to embrace the role whilst putting your own limitations around it.

By the time you get to the stage of having treatment with donated eggs, sperm or embryos you will have become very knowledgeable about fertility issues, treatment choices, the legal status and the short and long term implications

Telling and talking with family and friends about donor conception

of donor conception treatment…not to mention the emotional roller-coaster you have been travelling on. Unless you have been giving them a blow by blow account, most of your family and friends will have no idea of what you have been or are still going through. They need to catch up. They don't need to know everything but if they are going to be able to support you and your child then they need to know something.

Once you have shared some information with them, relatives and friends would ideally ask you what it is you need from them. If they don't ask first, think about how you can request the help or support you are looking for. It may not be easy to find a way to do this without causing some upset, but hopefully they will be pleased to know what your needs are and to be guided in their language and behaviour. Sometimes the educator role can evolve into that of counsellor as you find yourself needing to put yourself in their shoes and take into account their feelings when they first learn about donor conception. They may not have come across it before. After all, what you are looking for from them is as complex as the information you are conveying. There is mixed sadness and joy in the message you are giving them; what you may seek in their reaction is acknowledgement both of the difficulties you have been through and also the happiness in the situation you are now in. It is possible that sperm, egg or embryo donation may feel alien to them and until they understand more they could inadvertently make remarks that feel insensitive or judgemental.

One woman I talked to said,

"I was shocked when my mother said that the child I was carrying would not be her real grandchild, but then I realised that at first I had thought that an egg donation baby would not be my real baby. Her thinking was an extension of mine. Like me she needed time to think about what family and parenting means. Hopefully she will realise that family does not only have to mean genetic connectedness."

Just occasionally there are responses that are not directly negative but could require more attention. Avoidance and intense curiosity are examples.

Avoidance v curiosity

Some people just don't know what to say when told about donor conception. Older relatives in particular may be completely taken aback. If they understand what is being talked about – and confusion with non-donor in-vitro-fertilisation (IVF) often occurs – they may feel that it is a topic that is too intimate to be spoken about at all. They may appear not to understand in order to avoid the subject, or simply choose to ignore what is being said. There are various ways of responding to what is probably embarrassment but can feel like indifference. Do try to take into account the circumstances, context and feelings of your family member or friend, even if you had initially been looking to them for understanding your feelings.

Telling and talking with family and friends about donor conception

> Janet, whose daughter was conceived with help from a known egg donor, was, in her own words, 'very assertive' with both sets of grandparents. She insisted that they acknowledge their grand-daughter's beginnings and read the Telling and Talking booklets and appropriate Our Story book. She thinks that her husband's parents are accepting as they say, 'we just want you to be happy' and is certain that her mother is supportive and accepting. Sadly, her father has dementia and is unable to express a view. Perhaps what is more important is that both sets of grandparents clearly adore their grand-daughter.

> My husband and I took the path of least resistance when we told his family that the child I was carrying was conceived with help from a sperm donor. His parents lived in a small village, best described as conservative with both a large and small C. When Walter explained about his infertility and donor conception they appeared to understand but chose never to talk about it again. This behaviour was very typical of them and probably their class and generation. One simply did not talk about personal matters. We chose not to push them, particularly because, like Janet's family, their behaviour with our son was warm and loving. Sadly, they had both died by the time he would have been old enough to speak about his conception. If they had lived we would definitely have had to talk with them again.

In contrast to those who will do anything to avoid the subject, there are people who are fascinated by donor conception. Their curiosity can go beyond the bounds of showing that they care about you and stray into the intrusive and impertinent. It's almost as if the normal boundaries of the relationship have been lifted because you have shared something that is so personal.

> Solo mum Laura was shocked when she found herself embroiled in a conversation about the finances involved in donor conception when her neighbour started asking about why she hadn't paid off the mortgage on her house. She revealed much more than she wanted to and wished she had stopped earlier.

> Lesbian mum Ruth said that when her children were young, someone at a party started asking huge numbers of questions about whether she had had sex with the donor and whether she or her partner played 'dad' in the family.

It may be helpful for you to think in advance about what you will say if questions are asked that go beyond information you feel comfortable sharing. You may want to thank the questioner for their interest or concern but then put in place your own boundaries, possibly pointing out websites where they can get general information about donor conception or giving them a copy of *Our Family*, the companion booklet for relatives and friends.

When to tell

When to start sharing the information about the need for or use of donor conception is a very personal decision. It is also one that men and women may feel very differently about. At the risk of over-generalisation, typically women like to confide in other women. Sometimes a woman will have a very close relationship with her mother or a sister and cannot imagine not telling her about something so important in her life. But family relationships are not like this for everyone. Men tend to be more reticent about personal matters and compartmentalised in their lives. If the fertility issue is a male one then they may find it particularly difficult to talk about. All couples need to find a way to respect each other's changing needs to talk with selected others or retain privacy, particularly in the early days of diagnosis, decision making and treatment. At this stage the *Letter Leaflets* written by experienced parents to those just starting out can be very supportive. They are available on the DC Network website www.dcnetwork.org.

Deciding when to tell, as well as who needs to know and how to do it, is an important part of the planning for donor conception parenthood. Below are some of the pros and cons for telling at different stages, but first an issue that is raised by many parents whenever the issue of sharing information with children is talked about.

Telling others before the child understands

Potential or actual parents of donor conceived children very often wonder about whether they should or should not share information with others before the child is told. Many parents assume that the child should 'know' first and that the child should then be able to say who else should be told. This position feels very respectful of the child's privacy and right to own this information but there are a number of problems with it. The first is the difficulty of trying to pin down when a child actually 'knows'. The telling process may begin from infancy but a child rarely really understands what it means before the age of seven or so, although children of solo mums often grasp it earlier. It is unlikely that any child would be in a position to give their permission for others to be told until that sort of age. A child may, however, use some of the language that comes from one of the donor conception story books or has been used by parents, long before this time. If significant others have not been given information about the child's conception then there is a risk that they will either not believe the child, react negatively or feel upset that they had not been trusted by parents with the information.

There are two further problems with not telling others until the child understands. The first is that leaving it to children to share information as and when they feel appropriate may feel very burdensome for a child. They may be able to parrot the language but still only have a rough grasp of what it all means. They could also get the impression that this information is somehow more important than it should be, wondering why it is that others, particularly family members, don't know. A conclusion they could come to if others don't know or they have to give permission for others to know, is that there is something odd or wrong about donor conception and therefore about them. Additionally, it is also harder for parents to 'tell' the longer they have refrained from doing so, partly because they may be rusty with the language but also because it means admitting to misleading family members and friends over a long period.

Helen, who spoke at a DCN national meeting said –

"Am I worried that other people know about the egg donation before we told our girls? No – as I think that if we wait to tell them before we 'share' with anyone else that this might imply it is a secret rather than the story of their life...Don't get me wrong, I don't shout from the rooftops "I have undergone egg donation" and I would never share information with people unless the conversation was going in that direction but I am a very open person when it comes to the journey that we have taken to get our very special children."

It is just possible that the argument that children should know first is sometimes used when parents are uncomfortable or reluctant to share information with others because of unresolved feelings they have about donor conception. If, on thinking about it more, you feel this applies to you, then it may be helpful to seek some support and/or counselling. DC Network can help with this.

> "Two of the greatest fears I had about telling others were that I would be sharing information that wasn't mine to tell and that I would be judged for having children this way."
> *Amanda, mother to two donor conceived children*

Although this topic has never been researched, anecdotally DC Network has no evidence that young children mind others knowing about donor conception. For them it is just part of their story and, as indicated above, they might find it odd if others did not know. It can also be protective of children for important people in their lives, like teachers, to have a good understanding so that they can support a child if s/he chooses to speak in school about donor conception. This is particularly important for children in lesbian, gay or single mother families where absence of a father (or having two fathers or two mothers) is a difference that is noticed and commented on by other children.

Of course as children get older – and this can be anywhere between eight and twelve, depending on individual development and temperament, the challenge is to decide, with your child, when the information becomes theirs to share as they choose, rather than yours to share in their interest. For my family, and for many others, this happened at the secondary school transfer (age 11 to 12), with perhaps a period of parallel responsibility with regard to things like requests from doctors for information about family history.

Before treatment

To gain support some people like to tell one or two very close family members and/or friends almost from the start of knowing that help from a donor is going to be needed. These people may already know of your longing for a child and it may feel very natural to share this news with them. Hopefully they will be pleased that there is a way for you to have a family. However, others prefer to talk just with each other, if in a couple, at this stage and/or to seek the support of those who have faced similar questions and dilemmas through DC Network. Single women, in particular, often like the anonymous peer support to be found on fertility forums, such as DC Network's one for members only or a larger more public forum like Fertility Friends.

During treatment

Having decided to go ahead with donor conception, it can be very tempting to share the news widely with others. However, a potential downside to telling anyone during the treatment stage is that you may be asked regularly if you have any news, "Are you pregnant yet?". This can feel either caring or intrusive and burdensome, particularly if success is elusive. You may want to suggest that they will be the first to know if there is good news but in the meantime it would be helpful if they didn't ask (unless of course you would like them to). Occasionally some people find it necessary to withdraw from contact with certain relatives or friends for a while if they persist in asking questions or just don't 'get' the stress of going through fertility treatment.

Avoiding painful events

Something you may have been experiencing already, particularly if you have been trying to conceive for some time, is that Christmas (or other religious festivals) and events like weddings, baby showers and christenings can be very painful reminders of the child you long for. If you very understandably feel you would like to avoid, or spend just a short time at a celebration of this sort why not seek out the person most likely to be supportive and explain, without going into detail, that being around small children or pregnant women is difficult for you at the moment. If you think it is unlikely that the people organising the event will understand, simply make up a plausible excuse for your absence.

Pregnancy

Some people are more comfortable making the decisions privately and then sharing the news in pregnancy. This felt like the best of all possible options to Walter and me. We were able to grieve the child we could not have and move on to deciding that donor conception felt right, without being subject to other people's opinions and questions on the subject. When I became pregnant we were delighted to share the news with family and friends of what was a fait accompli by then. This gave everyone six or seven months to adjust to what was happening and be ready to welcome our baby into the world. Knowing about donor conception before the birth also meant that those close to us did not spend time speculating on who our son looked like…something that is a regular part of most new parent's lives.

Telling and talking with family and friends about donor conception

> Towards the end of her pregnancy Natasha and her husband Tim emailed close relatives to let them know which words they would and wouldn't be using to describe the donor and the act of donation and to encourage family members to avoid using particular phrases.
>
> Natasha found that the transition from infertility to standard ante-natal classes, which mainly involved mixing with people who had conceived with apparent ease, quite tricky. She made some good friendships but found it difficult to decide who to tell about her situation and how much information was appropriate. She found that it could be quite painful having conversations with class instructors and other would-be parents who all made assumptions of an easy conception and that this would also be so for second or subsequent babies.

Whilst ante-natal classes may prove a challenge you may more readily want to share information about donor conception with your midwife or obstetrician. If you have conceived by egg donation then the fact that the donor is (almost certainly) younger than you is important information when it comes to testing for chromosomal disorders. My own experience, and that of many others in all family types, is that the extra care that such a special pregnancy is often given feels nurturing and supportive. It is extremely rare for midwives or medics to make judgemental remarks about donor conception. Being open with them can be good practice for being open with others. But if you don't tell them you run the risk of repeating the experience of more than one egg donation parent: within seconds of the birth the midwife started commenting on the baby's features. "Well done, you've a lovely baby girl and she's got her mum's nose!" Not the best moment to face the issue of whether to tell.

After a child is born

All parents of new babies find relatives and strangers alike speculating about who the new family member looks like. Not only that, but more people than you might imagine will have an opinion on colouring, shape of nose, ears or eyes, amount of hair and the resemblance of these features to parents and other family members. Whilst people in the supermarket queue can be told anything you like, you may feel less comfortable avoiding or evading these questions from close relatives or friends.

Around the birth of a child is rarely an easy time to explain about donor conception because no matter how well you as parents have accepted needing a donor for family creation, it cannot be assumed that everyone else will instantly feel this way. As we have explored in this booklet, some people need time to catch up in their knowledge and understanding.

Whilst the need to tell someone new about donor conception will come up from time to time during your child's school years, it is likely to become harder and harder to share the information with those closest to you the longer time has passed. Relatives and friends with whom you are in contact on a daily or weekly basis may well wonder why you felt they could not be trusted with the information. Those able to put themselves in your shoes may feel sad about this but come to understand. Others may just feel deceived. Only you can know or anticipate how those closest to you are likely to respond, and the question of negative responses is addressed below. Although it may feel counterintuitive, by and large the news is kept in proportion if everyone important knows sooner rather than later.

Second stage telling

Many DC Network members have struggled with when to 'tell' friends they have made later, perhaps when their children start going to school or are joining sports or recreational clubs. Most have come to the conclusion that the same principles apply as with family and friends from earlier times. If someone is regularly in the life of your family, shares meals or holidays with you, and is likely to be around when donor conception issues come up naturally in conversation (such as talk about likenesses) then it is helpful that they should know. If a friendship reaches a level of closeness that you begin to feel that it is strange that these people do not know about how your family came into being, then it is probably time to tell. You know these people well by now so telling is likely to deepen the relationship; not-telling may get in the way of this happening. If friends find out later, or from others, they may wonder why you felt they could not be trusted with the information.

Who to tell

As indicated in the previous chapters it is close relatives and friends – those who will be continuing on life's journey with you – who need to know about donor conception. Other important people may be your family GP and your child's school. Many parents share information privately with each year group teacher in primary school so that they are in a position to believe and support a child should they choose to talk about donor conception.

When thinking about who needs to know, ask yourself, "Is it going to be in the interest of my child that this person knows?" The answer will be different for each family. It may be that the child-minder, baby-sitter or nursery should have the information or the parents of your child's best friend (and this will change as they get older) or other people who are important in your life. If they don't 'need to know' because they may not be around when your child talks about it, then there is no reason to tell them unless you wish to do so.

Some people find themselves blurting out the information to everyone they come across. Counsellor Ellen Glazer, co-author of *Having Your Child by Egg Donation*, feels that this kind of self-conscious telling may convey a sense of shame almost as much as secrecy does. In her American Fertility Association article, *'Talking with Family, Friends and Strangers about Infertility'* and in relation to donor conception Ellen says,

"Telling those who have no need to know may come across as more self-conscious and uncomfortable than honest and secure."

Ellen's experience, echoed by DC Network, is that those who tell all and sundry in the early days often regret it in the future and wish they had retained more privacy with acquaintances and strangers.

Telling and talking with family and friends about donor conception

Parents and very close friends are often the people that we turn to instinctively for support, although as we will see below parents can also be the people whose rejection or judgement we fear most.

> "It was very important to me that my parents were capable of answering questions around relatedness. I wanted back-up from them, particularly in relation to my sister and her children, Harry's cousins."
> *Catherine, mum to egg donor conceived son*

Relatives and close friends often feel very privileged to be included in the inner circle of knowledge about donor conception. They feel trusted and as a result are likely to be circumspect with the information, although it is helpful for you to indicate if it is all right for them to share the knowledge with others and how far this can go.

> Jennie was shocked when her brother introduced her as mother to an egg donation child at a social gathering where there were both people who knew and didn't know about donor conception. She wished she had been clearer with him from the start about how far the privileged information he had could be shared.

Surprisingly, people often do actually forget what they have been told and have been known to comment on physical likenesses that are a genetic impossibility.

DC Network member Claire says –

> *'We didn't want our children growing up in a conspiracy of secrets or a hierarchy of people knowing varying degrees of information at different times...We know that in being open we have to make some compromises about people knowing an intimate aspect of our life and information about our children, but we trust that we are doing our best."*
> *Quoted in Telling and Talking booklet for parents of children aged 0-7.*

Why might sharing information with family and friends sometimes feel so difficult?

Parents

It is very common to hear people contemplating donor conception talk about 'letting their parents down' – feeling they have somehow failed them by not being able to provide genetically connected grandchildren. They also sometimes worry that their parents will think a fertility issue in them, their adult child, reflects on their inheritance, care or upbringing and will blame themselves. The anxiety of anticipated parental sadness or worse still, judgement or rejection, is great. Single women, particularly from nuclear family backgrounds, can feel guilty about not following their parents in a conventional marriage, as well as sad about not having found a partner to have a child with. Lesbians may have to face family prejudice about their sexuality, which has been brought into sharper focus as a result of starting a family.

Letting go of the need for approval

Attached to our parents as we all are from infancy, pleasing them or not doing anything likely to upset them, feels important to most adults. We would prefer that they approve of the choices we make, but as adults we also need to be able to make decisions that are right for us as individuals and in our adult relationships. Balancing these two can sometimes feel tricky. One of the ways in which we demonstrate that we have separated from our parents is by taking responsibility for making decisions about which we inform, rather than consult, our parents. Hopefully, these choices are not made in a rebellious way but because we have come to have confidence in our ability to know what is right for us and go forward on that basis. Of course becoming separate from our parents does not mean the breaking of emotional ties. It simply means that we have fulfilled the aim of their parenting, that of bringing a child to a point in life where they are able to function well as an independent adult. If in adult life we still need full approval from our parents for everything we do, then it may be that there are complications with separation that could be helped by some counselling.

Recognising our parent's life experience

As we grow up and our parents grow older we often become protective of the older generation. As a result we can underestimate their experience of the world and their ability to deal with sorrow, difference and difficult choices. Being older does not necessarily mean being wiser, but many parents have had to manage feelings and events in their lives at least as mixed and difficult as using donor conception.

As adults themselves, your parents – and everyone else – are likely to take their cue from you. If you are confident and comfortable about the decisions you have made and convey this when you talk with them, then they are likely to be too.

Andrea, mother to an 18 year old sperm donor conceived daughter emailed me about the exercise around *Successes and Fears* that I ran at a DCN national conference.

"Successes: pretty much every example I could give you of telling family, friends, colleagues and professionals is of warm and interested responses. However, I think this is because of the way I tell – with confidence and security and not a smidgeon of self-doubt about using a donor."

Karen, mother to a sperm donor conceived daughter and Cristina, bisexual solo mum to sperm donor conceived twins, each initially wrote letters to their parents explaining about donor conception. Karen had anxieties stemming from her own strong Christian faith that was shared with her father and Cristina's dad lived in another culture many thousands of miles away. Both women stated in their letters that they would be telephoning in a few days to arrange to come and visit. In this way they were able to give as much information and reassurance as possible about what was happening before dealing with whatever initial reaction resulted. Cristina's father phoned within an hour of receiving her email to reassure her that he would support her in whatever way he could.

Siblings

Sometimes sibling relationships have been or remain competitive. If this is the case then perceiving that you may be seen as somehow 'less' in their eyes can be powerful. Maybe you are the eldest and your younger brothers and sisters are parents already. Your childlessness, or need for donor conception, can feel very painful in contrast. You may know or suspect that it is a source of family comment. Siblings can certainly be cruel. But some DC Network members have decided that brothers and sisters can make great allies, particularly when it comes to reinforcing information or influencing attitudes with parents or wider family.

> Janet found that her brother, with whom she had not been particularly good friends, was surprisingly supportive.

> Cristina, mentioned above, decided from the outset to include her two sisters in the education process she was going through herself. They were then able to be very supportive to her and helpful in facilitating their father's understanding about what was happening.

> Solo mum-to-be Rose told all her four siblings in different ways – face-to-face, email, telephone and letter. Her only sister followed up receipt of the letter with a swift phone call to convey that she was 'officially gobsmacked'. All four were supportive in their own ways but she enlisted her sister to help tell their mum.

Sibling relationships can also be affected by the choice of partner and the relationship with brothers- and sisters-in-law. These relationships can turn out to be happy and successful or full of jealousy and rivalry, and the way nephews and nieces are brought up can generate unspoken criticism and family tensions.

If you think your siblings (and their partners) may not be supportive, you may have to re-evaluate what they mean to you. Making clear that the decisions you have made have been fully thought through will be important.

If your brothers or sisters are parents already, their children will be cousins to yours. Your siblings will need advice on how you would like them to talk to their children about the donor conception of their cousins. So you will need to make your expectations clear as the cousins grow up. Give your siblings a copy of *Our Family*, the companion booklet to this one. Talking with children of relatives or friends is a topic addressed below.

Telling and talking with family and friends about donor conception

Friends

Unlike family, friends are people you choose to be in your life. They are your peers and most friendships flourish when the relationship is an equal one. Telling those friends you are close to can help deepen trust. They become people you can rely on. But it sometimes requires a deep breath to plunge into telling them something so intimate about your life.

> Ethan, devoted dad to sperm donor conceived twins, told me that sometimes when he tells friends about his children's conception he feels as if 'something is being taken away from me'. He explained that it felt like he was sharing something very intimate about himself that couldn't possibly be reciprocated by anyone else and it left him feeling slightly diminished. On balance, however, he said that sharing the information had added a level of intimacy and trust to friendships that had not been present before and he enjoyed this. Mixed and apparently contradictory feelings like Ethan's are very common.

> Chris, dad to two sperm donor conceived children, went out of his way to be up front with male friends about his infertility, utilising non-technical terms like shooting blanks, to his own advantage. This was a high risk strategy that required a lot of confidence but Chris was not one bit embarrassed about his infertility. His blunt and good humoured approach to talking with others won him admiration and a deeper relationship with friends. Humour can be used to keep others at arms length but in this case it was deployed to open up conversation.

> Solo mum Charlotte, pregnant and nearing her baby's birth when I spoke to her, had told a wide circle of friends about how she had conceived. Like many other single women in their late thirties Charlotte had taken a courageous decision that was recognised by friends, many of whom are around the same age. Some have been inspired by her, and others, whilst not feeling this would be their particular choice, are still very happy to support her.

> Peter and Sarah said that they had found it easier to talk with friends who, like themselves, have slightly 'different' families. They found that the bond of friendship deepened significantly when they shared information about the donor conception of their son with a couple who have an adopted child as well as a naturally conceived one.

As with family, the key to good support from friends is your confidence in the telling and letting them know what it is you need from them.

Telling and talking with family and friends about donor conception

Other children in the extended family or children of friends

Several of the parents I talked to as part of my research for both booklets were anxious about how to talk with cousins of their donor conceived children. Sometimes their siblings had asked what, if anything, they should say to their children.

Parents often fear that once a cousin realises that their uncle or aunt's child does not share a genetic connection, thoughtless or hurtful remarks may be made. This is unlikely to happen intentionally, unless there are other rivalries or jealousy involved. However, children can be very direct.

When talking with any child the most important factor to take into account is their stage of development, which may not be the same as their age in years. The principles are exactly the same as for sharing information with donor conceived children themselves. The *Telling and Talking* booklets, which are organised around children's developmental stages, could be of help here and you may want to direct your siblings or friends to them.

If cousins or children of friends are under five or six then it can be helpful for their parents to talk with them in a very general way about the different ways that families are made and that sometimes mummies and daddies need help from someone else to make a baby. Letting them know that a sperm and egg (or special cells) from a man and a woman are needed to make a baby is important too. When they have done this for a while, they can then say something along the lines of,

"And that's how your cousin Sammy was made. Aunty Jo needed an egg from another woman to help make him."

If the children being told are seven, eight or older when the donor conceived child comes on the scene, then a more direct approach may be required, although some talk about sameness and differences in other families they know can be helpful as well. Using a 'hook' provided by a child, as in the scenario below, can be a very natural way in to talking about donor conception and genetic relatedness. The opportunity, however, is unlikely to be presented in as direct a way in every family.

Catherine and Arthur were concerned that the very warm relationship between their nearly two-year-old egg donor conceived son Harry and his cousin's Max and Jack would be spoiled in some way if it was revealed that they were not genetically related. Max, at nearly nine, is science mad and Catherine was pretty sure that he would understand the non-genetic connection straight away should he learn about egg donation. She emailed me the following story of how the opportunity to share the information came up unexpectedly on a New Year's trip to the zoo.

Telling and talking with family and friends about donor conception

> "My sister and I had taken all the children to the zoo, but she had gone to get a cup of tea when Max said out of the blue, 'I share 50 per cent of my genes with Harry because you and Mummy are sisters.' I said to both Max and Jack that this would usually be the case but in our family it was a bit different. I went on to explain that we had tried to have a baby for many years and that I had lots of tests and finally the doctors had told me that my eggs weren't working properly. Max was very interested in what that actually meant and wanted details! I said that a very kind lady in America gave us some eggs and that they were fertilised with Arthur's sperm to produce embryos. Max was very interested in how many embryos and that it was Arthur's sperm so that he was genetically related to Harry. He also wanted to know how they put the embryos back into my tummy. He then said something along the lines of, "So that lady is Harry's genetic mummy." I said yes, they do share their genes, but he grew in my tummy and I gave birth to him and look after him so I'm his Mummy. He seemed to think that was perfectly OK.
>
> Max's little brother Jack then piped up and said, "If that kind lady hadn't given you her eggs, then you and Uncle Arthur wouldn't have been able to have a baby and we wouldn't have our cousin Harry." I agreed and said no more on the subject. When my sister re-appeared with her tea Max was very keen to explain what he had discovered and when we got home he also said, "Daddy, daddy, guess what..." and launched into the same story, although became distracted half way through.
>
> Since then Max hasn't talked about it except when we were talking about whether we can all roll our tongues. He and Jack both know it is inherited and that I can and Arthur can't roll our tongues. Max was asking if Harry could and I said it was too early to know yet. He thought about it and said maybe he wouldn't be able to unless the donor could.
>
> Both Max and Jack's behaviour towards Harry is no different and neither have asked further questions since New Year's Day. I am sure they will in their own good time. It wasn't the ideal location to discuss Harry's background but I'm so glad it came up so naturally."

Of course this heart-warming story was only possible because Catherine had a very good relationship with her sister, who had always been supportive of her and was happy for her sons to know about egg donation. It also took a lot of confidence on Catherine's part to be able to take up the opportunity offered by Max's out-of-the-blue question. She had no shame about the way that Harry had been conceived and was only concerned about the future of the relationship between the children. She had instinctively felt that this would be promoted by early transparency about egg donation, but had been anxious about how to start the conversation and how the news would be received.

If I tell others how can I control the information?

The simple answer is that you can't. Once you have told, you can't untell, although remarkably people often do forget, indicating that the information is not necessarily as earth shattering as we might think it is. You cannot directly control other people's behaviour but by being clear about your own needs, wishes and behaviour you can put in place some boundaries. For instance, you can ask those you tell to talk to you before they share the information with someone else. Hopefully, this will make them stop and think first. You might want to explain about the difference between secrecy and privacy. The fact that they have been told means that the information is not secret, but it is as private as knowledge of how anyone has conceived a child. Good friends often feel privileged to have been told and this makes them circumspect about sharing the facts with others.

There is some anecdotal evidence within DC Network that telling quite a wide circle of those who might value knowing in a low key, matter-of-fact way puts the information in proportion. It is something worth communicating but not making a huge fuss about. Members have found that this strategy often works much better than telling a select few but indicating that it is highly confidential and should not be shared. Being asked to keep a secret seems to trigger in some people a desperate need to tell others, resulting in rumour and school-gate chat.

How wide the information about donor conception goes is a matter of personal choice, but if you feel 'stuck' around this issue it may be worth asking yourself the questions, 'Why does it really matter if others know?' and 'What is the worst that can happen?' Honest answers could help you acknowledge some fears that have still to be addressed and hopefully this booklet may help with.

Not many people would choose to be as open as Walter and I have… appearing on TV and in national newspapers from time to time, but at no point over the last 30 years have we been subject to any negative or judgemental remarks.   What about our children you may be wondering? Our daughter has always been proud of her 'difference' in being donor conceived and talks with anyone about it if the topic comes up. We stopped doing publicity at our son's request when he was a young teenager and wanted to be just like his mates, but both our children, now adults, are very supportive of what we do and our confidence around donor conception. It has helped them feel proud of who they are too.

Once my child knows can I have any influence over who s/he tells?

Again the answer is no, which is why it is important that those who are close to a child, or in a position to support them and influence others, know.

The experience in DC Network is mostly that young children do not talk about donor conception. Children of solo mums or lesbian mothers may do so because they are asked about having a dad. The subject is not **not** talked about because it is upsetting or worrying in any way, but simply because they don't really understand and as such it is not interesting. Some small children do use some of the language from the story books with friends but as other children don't understand what they are talking about, the topic gets changed very quickly. Older children who try to explain about donor conception can become quite frustrated by the lack of understanding by friends who either think they are a 'test tube baby', adopted or an orphan.

> Karen, who had not been hugely open about sperm donation with anyone but very close family, was surprised when she found that her seven year old daughter had told her babysitter. Karen talked with the sitter and was relieved to find that the news was accepted with interest but without fuss, which gave her confidence to be more open with others.

It is around the age of seven and older that children gain a much clearer understanding of donor conception and may want to raise the topic in class when talk turns to biology and inheritance of characteristics. If a child is confident and comfortable about their beginnings – and many DC children are rather proud of their 'difference' – then they are mostly well able to manage the questions and remarks that other children may make.

All parents feel very protective about their children and parents of donor conceived children sometimes worry a lot about bullying taking place because of their 'difference'. Of course perceived difference of any sort can provide the potential for bullying. As a parent, what can be difficult to identify is what is teasing – something that is part and parcel of social relationships and often a form of affection – and bullying. Children's relationships often move on very swiftly (best friends one day, enemies next week) so bullying can be fleeting, difficult to recognise and name. If, however, it becomes clear that this is happening then it should be dealt with in the same way as bullying of any sort; reassurance for the child, talking to teachers if it is in school, talking to other parents outside of school and making sure the school's policy is being followed.

Children of solo mums and lesbian couples can find that they are the focus of intense questioning, sometimes amounting to bullying, around the issue of whether or not they have a dad. This is addressed in the section below. Parents in heterosexual couples have not reported incidences of their children being bullied to DC Network.

If you live in a community or your child attends a school where information about donor conception may not be well received, then from the age of seven or eight children can understand that not everyone needs to know. You could talk with them about some things being private to your family. But this strategy does risk giving a child a mixed message about donor conception and you should be very clear that it is not led by your anxiety about being exposed in some way. How you talk with your child, as much as what you say, is likely to be the key to successfully establishing any necessary limits on who your child tells, without them feeling that donor conception is something that has to be hidden.

It can be helpful for parents to look at the school curriculum and/or talk with teachers about when biology and human reproduction are going to be introduced. This is so that you can mention it to your child in advance and to try and make sure that all types of assisted conception are covered as ways of making a baby. Even if your child does not want to speak about their own situation it can be helpful for them to have their method of conception acknowledged and normalised. Of course teachers need to be sensitive in their handling of this topic, not pointing out children they know are donor conceived, but prior knowledge of who they are may prevent teachers making inappropriate remarks or tolerating such remarks by other pupils.

> Natasha, daughter of a solo mum, telling her story in *The Guardian* newspaper, said that, age 11, she pointed out to teachers that sex was not the only way that babies were made.

Solo mums and lesbian couples: when family type is the dominant issue

Children of solo mums and lesbian couples do sometimes find themselves being quizzed by other children, not so much about donor conception directly, but about whether or not they have a dad. These children can be persistent to the point of bullying and beyond a certain time cannot be fobbed off by the donor conceived child saying, "We are a mum and kids family" "We don't have a dad in our family" or "We have two mums, two grannies and Uncle George".

The difficult time is when children are too young to be interested in the mechanics of fertility treatment but may be questioned by slightly older children who know very well that both a man and a woman have to be involved somehow in the making of a baby. It can be helpful if the donor conceived child has a basic understanding that if a woman doesn't have all the ingredients to make a baby then these can be obtained from a hospital. However, it is also very reasonable for a child to say, 'If you don't believe me, ask my mum' or in modern parlance, 'Google it'.

Solo mum Lucy and her son Charlie, age six, dealt with questioning this way.

"A classmate asked Charlie about his dad and he replied that we don't have a dad in our family, it's mummy and me, to which his questioner said, 'You must have'. Charlie gave the same answer and added that there are lots of different types of family, some live with their dad, some with grannies and granddads and my family is mummy and me. The classmate said, 'But you must have a dad or you wouldn't exist'. Another child then joined in, saying 'Is it true that you don't have a dad?' Charlie said that it was true and the second child responded with, 'Ugh, that's weird'. Charlie then felt unable to go into the donor situation although he has all the answers.

I tried role playing with Charlie about how he might answer, but in the end we agreed that he would tell them to speak to me if they asked again. Luckily, I do pick him up several times a week so this is feasible."

Lucy is planning to speak to the teacher to see if something about different family types can be included in the children's learning, in the hope that this may satisfy the other children for a while.

Telling and talking with family and friends about donor conception

> In the *Telling and Talking* booklet for parents of young children, Gwyneth talks about her daughter Helen being questioned in a similar way. Eventually, the form teacher read the book Our Story for children in single parent families to the class, demonstrating to them that she supported Helen and her different family story. It effectively stopped other children pestering her about a dad.

> Elisabeth, solo mum to two sons aged four and two, believes that directness on her part, combined with good explanations in simple language, have given her oldest son a good understanding of donor conception and the confidence to talk about it. He is happy to tell anyone that he has a 'donor dad' rather than a 'real dad'. Elisabeth started to use the term 'donor dad' because a friend of hers with a donor conceived child used it with her daughter and she thought it would be helpful if all the children used the same language. Now she has discovered that there is a donor conceived child in her son's class whose mother, being anxious to avoid any hint of a family relationship, has given her son the term 'biological donor' to use. Elisabeth is now thinking of introducing this way of referring to the donor to her son so that he can share language with this child who seems to be becoming a friend.
>
> Elisabeth is a very open person and it would appear that her sons are happy to follow suit. She has not yet found, and may never find it necessary to ask her sons to refer questioners to her. She will, however, be checking as the boys grow up that information fed to her youngest son by her eldest is correct!

As many solo mums work full time, a lot of their children's social interaction takes place without them. One mum suggested that it's a good idea to prepare children for the fact that lots of people don't know that you can have children without a daddy. "My mummy didn't know this till she asked the doctor." Another mum's daughter succinctly responded with the phrase, "Actually you *can*" (emphasis on the last word) when told it wasn't possible to have a baby without a daddy.

It seems that equipping children with a range of possible answers, knowledge appropriate for their understanding, useful terminology and lots of confidence are keys to responding to questions about the existence of a dad. That, and giving children permission to set their own limits by saying "It's private", "Nobody's business", "I don't want to talk about it" or "Talk to my mum", if they don't want to respond or are feeling under pressure.

Children conceived through egg donation or embryo donation are less likely to be asked questions about their female donor by other children at a very young age as this is not immediately visible in the same way. However other children may become aware of it at some point. Again children will respond to this in different ways. Some may not need any help. For others some parental/teacher/adult intervention, support and explanation may help.

As was said earlier, giving children the confidence to answer these questions or to seek support from an adult when required seems the way forward. Providing teachers with educational material on family differences at an appropriate time can also be considered, although this requires being open with the school and solo mums may not always feel this is possible for a variety of reasons. In reality, if you ask 10 solo mums how they would handle these situations, each would have a different approach. Ultimately it's about navigating the journey of conversations with other children in a way that is right for your family and accepting that this may change and evolve as your child grows up.

How much to tell

There are a lot of questions you may find yourself being asked – how much do you know about the donor? Did you have much choice about the donor? Where did you have your treatment? How long did it take you to conceive? How much did it cost? Who else knows? – and many more. What you say in answer to any of these may depend on whether you view the question as a reasonable one or not, how much information there is to share and if the questioner is a person you want to have the information anyway. As discussed earlier some people can be very inquisitive and it is best to think about and to decide what boundaries you want to put and whether there are any facts or details you definitely won't want to share. Many parents feel that information about the donor's background, his/her pen portrait and certainly the 'letter to the child' if there is one, belongs to their child to share if they choose to do so in the future. It is perfectly reasonable just to say that you know some of his or her physical characteristics, even if you are one of the lucky ones to have considerably more information.

> Jen, a lesbian solo mum, found that her son's kindergarten were so interested in her situation that they asked if she would be willing to give a talk to other parents. As her son had only just started she said she would let him settle first and then think about doing this later.

Parents with a donor who is personally known to them are sometimes cautious about letting this be known, worrying that it may stimulate curiosity they do not wish to satisfy. Some people find it hard to imagine a situation where a donor is a family member or friend and can unthinkingly make remarks that reveal their discomfort. This is not inevitable of course.

> Ruth, a lesbian mum to two sons, has been happy to explain to those who want to know, that her donor is the husband of a friend and that he sees the boys three or four times a year, but is not involved in their lives on a day to day basis.

Telling and talking with family and friends about donor conception

> Janet's egg donor is her old friend Lesley. She used to live close by but is now about 60 miles away. She was guest of honour at Janet's son Ben's naming ceremony but now sees the family about twice a year. Lesley has said that she feels a link to Ben but he doesn't feel like hers. Janet and Lesley, who are both quite open people, are very grateful for the excellent counselling they received at the clinic where they felt that the interests of all the children involved were constantly held in mind. Lesley is mother to four children.

If a donor is actually a co-parent with a lesbian couple or single woman or is otherwise involved with the child, then it is helpful for you to explain the situation to those who need to know. It may be particularly useful to share the name or term by which the donor is known to the child. Sharing the parental name of the non-birth mother in lesbian families with important others is also valuable so that she can be acknowledged by teachers, for instance, as being the other parent in the child's life.

Reflections on telling

The vast majority of DCN members who took part in the exercise on *Fears and Successes* at the DCN national conference said that their worries about talking with friends and family had not been realised. One solo mum reported that 'telling friends and family gave me a sense of liberation and freedom', and a mum by egg donation said, "All positive, people are lovely and more enlightened now". Often the news of donor conception was received with interest and sometimes curiosity, but then forgotten about.

> "I couldn't believe it when it became obvious that my best friend had completely forgotten. This wasn't because he didn't place any importance on me sharing a personal matter but because he didn't see it as relevant to me being a father."
> *Ethan, dad to sperm donor conceived twins*

> Claire, quoted in the section on Who to Tell, whose two sperm donor conceived children are now older teenagers, said that she was so pleased they had chosen to be open with others right from the start. No member of her family had ever been on the receiving end of judgemental or unkind remarks.

Not everyone of course had such overwhelmingly positive experiences. A solo mum said that it took about five or six months for her family to 'warm up', but others were very supportive. A mother by egg donation reported that her mother had completely accepted her granddaughter, but had been totally unsupportive during the treatment phase. Another egg donation mum said that she had been taken aback by the negative reaction from a strongly Christian friend and was now cautious about who she told. Her father, however, had always been there for her.

It is interesting that in research conducted by the Morgan Centre at Manchester University into experiences of sharing donor conception information in heterosexual couples and lesbian families, that grandparents found it very difficult to criticise decisions made by their adult children. They clearly had strong feelings about infertility and donor conception and had experienced with sadness the ripples of distress coming from the infertile couple, but were very loyal in their unwillingness to comment adversely. Of course parents of heterosexual couples have assumptions of eventual grandparenthood that is not shared by parents of lesbians who have mostly assumed that they could not have expectations in this direction. Announcements of pregnancy in lesbian couples were almost universally greeted with delight, but huge surprise.

When the response is negative

The underlying theme of this booklet is that conveying information about donor conception with confidence but without fuss is likely to bring about mostly positive responses. But be prepared for the unexpected; take it slowly and listen out for how the news is going down. Even people who mean well can get it badly wrong at first.

If your need for donor conception is infertility, some people will want to start by expressing deep sympathy for your misfortune. Or they immediately focus on some negative aspect: "Goodness, it won't be easy for you, bringing up a child you're not related to." This is probably not what you are looking for, if in your mind you are hoping to share joyful news of a pregnancy. Others may just make light of the difficulties you've been through and brush these aside: "Well done you! Lots of people have fertility problems these days, so it's nothing special".

Some people may make unthinking and what feel like insensitive comments when first told but be open to learning more (see section on becoming an educator). But what about when this doesn't happen, when a relative or friend is persistently negative, either in words or behaviour, even after they have had time to get used to the idea? This can be much harder of course when it is a close relative rather than a friend who is behaving this way. It is sad to lose friends but if they cannot respect the decisions you have made about creating your family then maybe they are not the people you thought they were. For many it is much more distressing, emotionally and practically, to leave a close relative behind.

Thinking back to the section on why sharing information with family might feel so difficult, it seems it is parents who could be the main stumbling block here. They are our children's grandparents – or will be – and many of us find ourselves becoming much closer again to our own parents with the common experience of bringing up a family. When it is the very creation of this family that seems to be causing the difficulties, the feelings can be very painful.

It is unlikely that negativity about donor conception will have come out of the blue. There will have been earlier clues, perhaps rather inflexible views about social change in the modern world, a reluctance to acknowledge you as a grown-up, resistance to change in general or a personality that has

Telling and talking with family and friends about donor conception

proved difficult in the past. Or there may be deeply held religious beliefs that a grandparent finds hard to reconcile with a child coming into the family by donor conception. Unless the religious beliefs are very rigid, it may be easier to appeal to the goodness in someone who has a strong faith. They may be able to find in their hearts the capacity to combine respect for the decisions their adult child has made with the love of their God. People with a history of difficult behaviour or resistance to change may be much more fixed in their views and therefore much harder to bring round.

> Karen's father, a clergyman, struggled with the idea that his daughter would be, as he saw it, carrying another man's child. He actually said this on the phone to Karen's husband, who was himself perfectly comfortable with sperm donation. Karen could see that her father was having a very hard time with the idea but at the same time his love for her was evident and tangible as well. When Karen became pregnant he was quiet but supportive. He has completely accepted and adores his grand-daughter. Karen still finds it easier to have conversations with her mum than her dad.
>
> In the book *Making Finn*, Roxi, one half of a lesbian couple, dreads having to tell her strictly Christian parents about her partner's pregnancy by donor sperm. Her parents know, in theory, about their daughter's sexuality but they have never had to confront it before. They are very shocked when Roxi finally stumps up the courage to tell them the news. It looks at first as if they are not going to be supportive but come round after Roxi explains about how difficult it was for her being raised in such a rigid household, particularly as she became aware in her teenage years of her sexuality.

Babies often bring love with them. It is a rare grandparent, uncle or aunt who can resist being part of the admiring circle around a new-born or the smiley charm of a one year old. But from time-to-time difficult decisions may have to be made. Just occasionally, and very sadly, the only thing parents can do is either marginalise or cut a persistently negative person out of their life. It is an action of last resort but if there is danger of that person ignoring or treating differently (to other grandchildren for instance) a donor conceived child, then contact is not going to benefit them.

> "We knew in our hearts that donor conception was right for us, so when Jim's dad was so negative we decided we would see him at weddings and funerals, but not otherwise. We are sad about it but the big loss is his not ours."
> *Janis, mum to sperm donor conceived twins.*

Explaining to children why the family does not see a relative – and grandparents are particularly difficult – may not be easy. Until a child is old enough to understand that the world is made up of people with lots of different points of view, it may be simpler not to draw attention to the lack of contact. Very young children will not know any different and if, as they get to seven or eight, they ask you can say something along the lines of,

"People don't always see eye to eye in families. Granddad doesn't really understand about donor conception and we don't agree about it. At the moment I/we've decided it's best if we don't meet up. I'm sad that he's missing out on having a good time with you when he doesn't need to, and I hope he will realise that... maybe when you get a bit older."

Put this way it shows that you as a parent are taking responsibility for making the decision (so your child doesn't feel responsible) and that it is clear that it's Granddad who has to change.

Final thoughts

It might be easy to believe that being open about donor conception with friends and family is the right thing to do. Putting openness into action can be more difficult, and fears of stigma or rejection remain strong. The good news is that they are not often realised.

"We were very worried that our parents would disapprove of donation and that there would be bonding issues as well. These proved completely irrational! Total acceptance by all."
DC Network member Bob taking part in the Fears and Successes exercise.

It is probably best to expect to feel a little wobbly when you first talk about donor conception, but to know that your confidence and comfort with the choices you have made will set the tone for how most people will respond. Taking charge, planning when and what you want to say and how you will say it, will help give you that confidence.

Telling and talking with family and friends about donor conception

Dos and Don'ts

Do

- Tell with confidence but without fuss. Matter-of-fact explanations help keep donor conception in proportion and discourage gossip.

- Let family and friends know what you need from them.

- Become an educator, but decide on your own boundaries around this role.

- Try not to take offence or get upset if people make unthinking or insensitive remarks at first. They may be open to learning more and you can help them.

- Put yourself in the shoes of older relatives or others who may not have encountered donor conception before and may be unsure if they want to talk about it.

- Give your relatives and friends copies of the parallel booklet *Our Family*, which is intended for them.

Don't

- Start to tell people before you've thought about or agreed how much information you are going to share

- Feel bad, when you are going through treatment, about turning down invitations to events where there will be pregnant women or small children. Explain beforehand that this is something you can't manage at the moment. If you think you are not going to be understood, simply make up a plausible excuse.

- Think that everyone has to be told. As long as the inner circle of people who know include those travelling on life's journey with you, as well as professionals supporting or treating your child, those relatives or acquaintances in outer circles have no need to know.

Telling and talking with family and friends about donor conception

Resources

Books

- Ken Daniels,
  Building a family with the assistance of donor insemination
  (Dunmore Press, Palmerston North, 2004)
  Available in the UK only from DC Network

- Ellen Sarasohn Glazer and Evelina Weidman Sterling,
  Having your baby through egg donation, Second Edition
  (Jessica Kingsley, London, June 2013)

- Diane Ehrensaft, *Mommies, daddies, donors, surrogates: answering tough questions and building strong families*
  (The Guildford Press, New York, London, 2005)

- Susan Newham-Blake,
  Making Finn: one couple's unconventional journey to motherhood
  (Penguin South Africa 2013)

- Olivia Montuschi,
  Telling and Talking booklets, 0-7, 8-11, 12–16, 17+
  (Donor Conception Network, 2006, 0-7 updated 2012, 8-11 updated 2013)
  Printed and pdf copies available from www.dcnetwork.org

- Olivia Montuschi,
  Mixed Blessings: Building a family with and without donor help
  (Donor Conception Network 2012)
  pdf copies only available from www.dcnetwork.org

- *Our Story* children's story books for all family types available from Donor Conception Network, www.dcnetwork.org

Films

- *A Different Story* (Donor Conception Network, 2003) DVD.
  Seven children and young people from heterosexual couple families talk about their thoughts and feelings about being conceived with the help of anonymous sperm donors. Available to buy or borrow from DC Network library.

- *Telling and Talking about Donor Conception*
  (Donor Conception Network 2006) DVD.
  Parents and children talk about their experiences of telling. Includes solo mums and a lesbian family.
  Available to buy or borrow from DC Network library.

Research on sharing information with others

- *Relative Strangers project*
  conducted by Professor Carol Smart and Dr. Petra Nordqvist at the Morgan Centre, University of Manchester
  March 2013
  http://www.socialsciences.manchester.ac.uk/morgancentre/research/relative-strangers/

  This research project explored how heterosexual and lesbian couples who conceive using donor sperm, eggs or embryos negotiate telling parents and relatives about their decision to use a donor. Wider family is often very important in the context of having a baby, and the project investigated how couples feel about sharing information about the process of donor conception with their own parents, in-laws, extended families and of course their children.

  As part of this project heterosexual and lesbian couples, and also grandparents of donor conceived children, were interviewed about their experiences.

- Petra Nordqvist has also written extensively on lesbian parenthood here: www.socialsciences.manchester.ac.uk/morgancentre/research/relative-strangers/outputs/index.html.

- Nuffield Council on Bio-Ethics
  Report on Donor Conception: Ethical aspects of information sharing
  April 2013
  www.nuffieldcouncilonbioethics/donor-conception

  This report explores the ethical issues that arise around the disclosure of information in connection with donor conceived people.

Organisations

British Association for Counselling and Psychotherapy
15 St. John's Business Park
Lutterworth
Leicestershire
LE17 4HB
01455 883300
www.bacp.co.uk
bacp@bacp.co.uk

British Infertility Counselling Organisation (BICA)
Website, including Find a Counsellor facility:
www.bica.net
info@bica.net

Donor Conception Network
154 Caledonian Road
London
N1 9RD
020 7278 2608
www.dcnetwork.org
enquiries@dcnetwork.org

Human Fertilisation and Embryology Authority
10 Spring Gardens
St James's
London
SW1A 2BU
020 7291 8200
www.hfea.gov.uk
admin@hfea.gov.uk

Facing Parenthood
http://www.facing-parenthood.com/whoweare.htm

A specialist service offering help with the emotional and relationship challenges of fertility, pregnancy, birth and parenthood.

Based in N. London but accessible to all via telephone counselling.
Tel: 020 8444 9160

Natalie Gamble – Solicitor
Natalie Gamble Associates
19 Glasshouse Studios
Fryern Court Road
Burgate
Nr. Salisbury
Wiltshire
SP6 1QX
www.nataliegambleassociates.com
Natalie@nataliegambleassociates.com
0844 357 1602

Useful websites

Donor Sibling Registry (DSR)
https://www.donorsiblingregistry.com/

The largest and most comprehensive site for connecting donor offspring donors/half-siblings. Started in the US by Wendy Kramer and her sperm donor conceived son Ryan, it has many entries for UK clinics. In addition to the registry there is an excellent section giving access to up to date research and many ways of connecting with and exploring donor conception issues with others.

Choice Moms.org
www.choicemoms.org

Single Mothers by Choice
www.singlemothersbychoice.org

The two websites above are well-respected, long-standing American organisations for single women who are choosing to become solo mothers.

Fertility Friends
UK based: the largest and best used public infertility/fertility forum
www.fertilityfriends.co.uk

American Fertility Association
http://www.theafa.org/about-the-afa/

A counsellor-led not-for-profit organisation providing supportive and educational materials for anyone looking to build a family and experiencing infertility and/or the need for donated gametes. Inclusive of all family types, this organisation has some excellent short leaflets and podcasts on many aspects of family creation by donor conception.

The Donor Conception Network

The Donor Conception Network provides support and resources to anyone who is thinking about using or who has used egg, sperm or embryo donation to have children. We work directly with families and donor conceived people but also advocate on their behalf, advising clinics, policy makers and other professional bodies.

We are primarily a membership organisation offering contact, community, support and information to donor conception families around the world. Our members range from people at the very early stages of thinking about donor conception to those with adult children now having families of their own.

Our website also provides a wealth of information and guidance. We have an online shop selling books and films for donor conception families including books for young children – the *Our Story* range – and our new book for 8–12yr olds *"Archie Nolan: Family Detective"*.

We publish our Journal twice a year, have a monthly newsletter, run two family conferences in the UK for members each year as well as organising a range of local groups all around the UK. We also offer online contact to members who don't live in the UK or near a local group. We run workshops for those considering donor conception as well as Telling and Talking Workshops for those who have children. Our range of books will continue to expand as our resources allow.

Most importantly we work hard to ensure that donor conception families are represented, their voices are heard, and that donor conception is openly understood by the wider community as one of many ways a family can be created or expanded.

Donor Conception Network

Join us to be part of an organisation proudly supporting and championing you and families like yours.

For information about membership or to make a donation towards our work please visit our website.

CPSIA information can be obtained
at www.ICGtesting.com
Printed in the USA
BVHW022211310822
646046BV00012B/78